Usborne

Starting School

sticker book

D1099051

Illustrated by Kay Widdowson

Designed by Stephanie Jones

Words by Felicity Brooks

Getting ready to go

Jack and Martha are getting ready to go
to school. Can you help them get dressed?

Jack

Martha

Jack's backpack

Put Jack's book, pencil case, drink and snack in his backpack. Put his toy car in too.

At the pegs

At school, everyone hangs up their coats and bags. Martha and Jack have put their things under their names. Put the other children's things in the right places.

Jack

Oliver

Ella

Ruby

Martha

Joshua

Can you put Martha's
shoes on for her?

5

In the classroom

In the classroom, the teacher calls out all the childre[n] [and m]ake sure everyone is there. P[ut the] children on the mat and add tic[ks to the tea]cher's register.

Add a tick to the register after you put each child on the mat.

Class register

Ella ✔   Martha ✔

Jack ✔   Oliver ✔

Joshua ✔   Ruby ✔

Numbers and shapes

These children are playing with shapes and numbers. Can you finish the number and shape charts?

| Square | Circle | Rectangle | Triangle | Star |

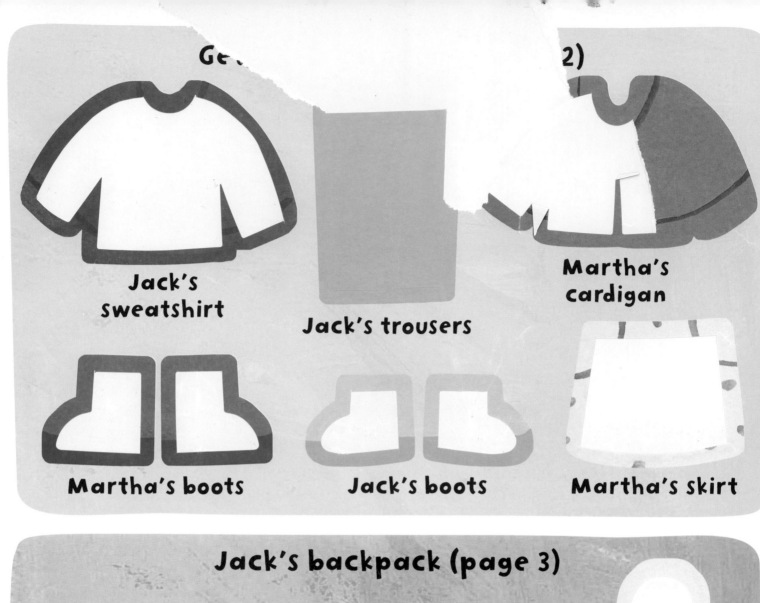

Get **~2)**

Jack's sweatshirt

Jack's trousers

Martha's cardigan

Martha's boots

Jack's boots

Martha's skirt

Jack's backpack (page 3)

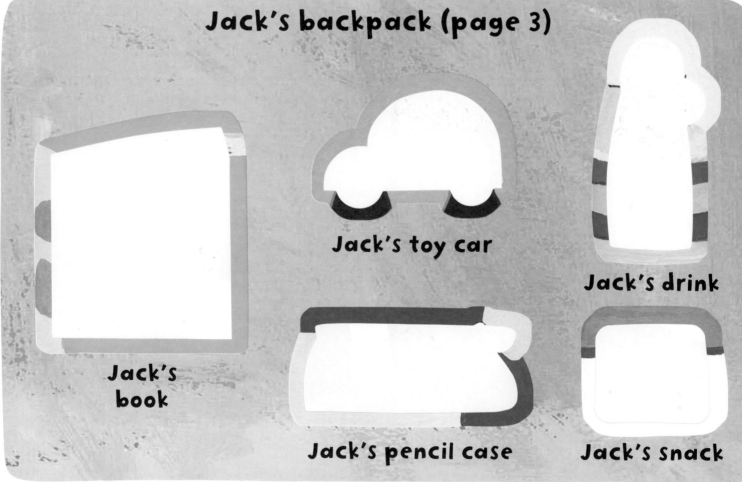

Jack's book

Jack's toy car

Jack's drink

Jack's pencil case

Jack's snack

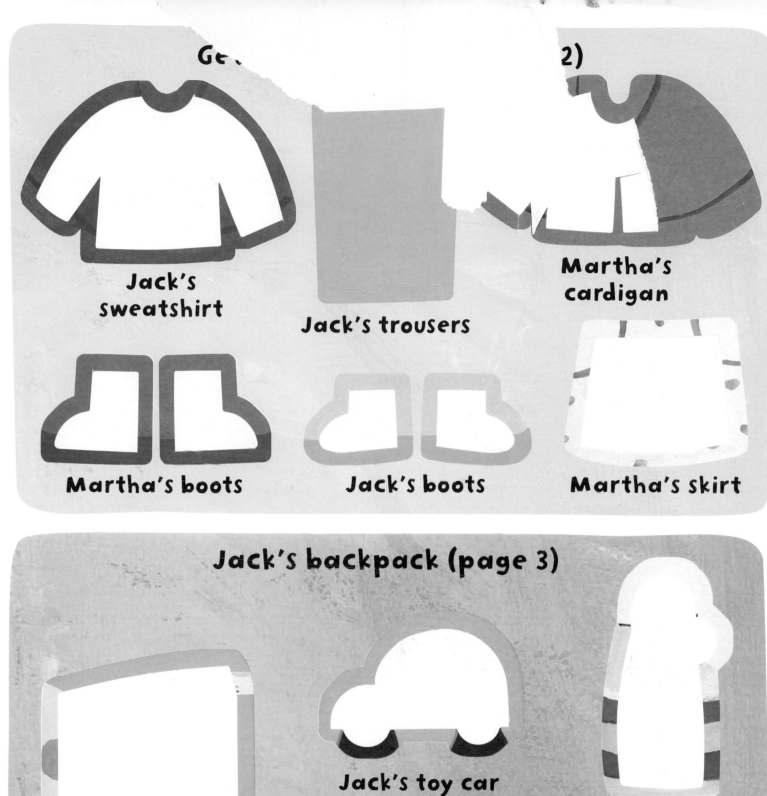

Ge... 2)

Jack's sweatshirt

Jack's trousers

Martha's cardigan

Martha's boots

Jack's boots

Martha's skirt

Jack's backpack (page 3)

Jack's book

Jack's toy car

Jack's drink

Jack's pencil case

Jack's snack

Home time

When it is time to go home, everyone puts on their coats and finds their things. Help Martha and Jack get ready to go home.

Books

n o p q r s t u v w x y z

Storytime

The teacher is reading the children
a story about a dragon and a princess.
Jack and Martha are acting the story.
Can you put on their costumes?

Can you finish this alphabet line?

a b c d e f g h i j k l m

Colours

Red   Green   Brown   Pink   Black

Yellow   Blue   Purple   Orange   White

Give Martha and Jack some crayons, glue, scissors and paper.

Art time

Ruby and Joshua are doing some painting. Give them each an apron and a paintbrush. Can you add the colour stickers to the colour chart too?

Easel

Put a painting on the easel and add some more paint pots.

Lunchtime

Choose some food to put in Martha and Jack's lunchboxes. Ella is having a hot lunch. Put a knife and fork on the table for her and put some food on her plate.

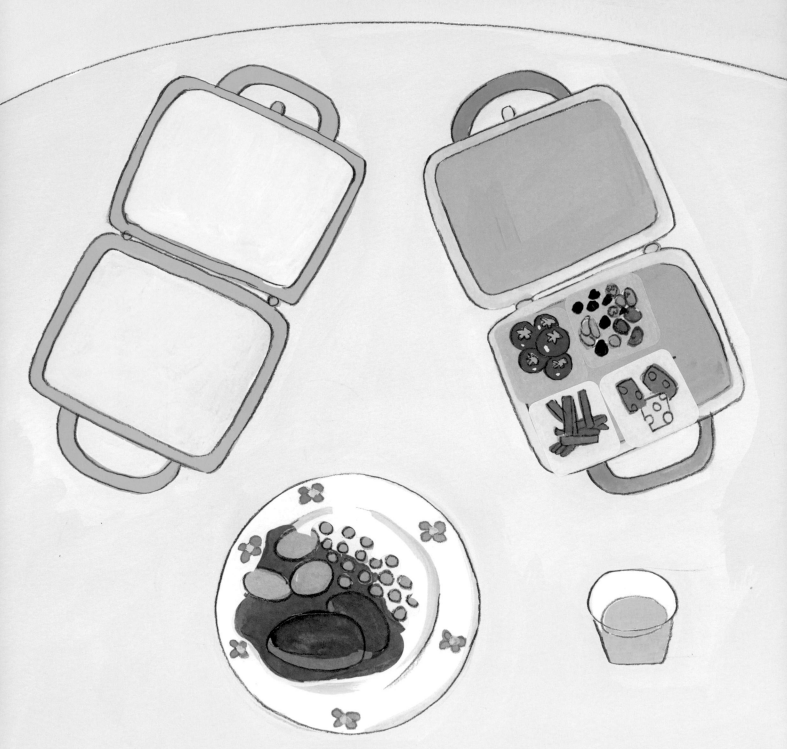

Time for PE

It's time to do PE. Can you help Jack and Martha put on their PE clothes?

Playtime

At playtime, everyone plays outside.
Put some toys in the sandpit and add
some more children to the picture.

Home time (page 16)

bird

Jack's hat

Martha's earmuffs

bird

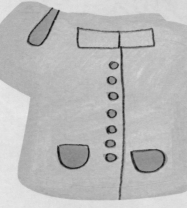

Jack's coat

Martha's coat

Jack's scarf

Martha's scarf

bird

Jack's backpack

Martha's backpack

football

Jack's boots

Martha's boots

g h i j k l m
n o p q r
s t u v w

alphabet letters

book

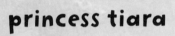

princess tiara

teddy
bear

dragon head

princess dress

books

princess slippers

dragon body

dragon feet

Art time (pages 12 and 13)

crayons

scissors

paper

pink

glue

black

yellow

brown

purple

blue

green

crate

paint pots

orange

paintbrushes

aprons

painting

Time for PE (page 10)

Jack's T-shirt

Jack's shorts

Martha's sweatshirt

Martha's tracksuit bottoms

Jack's trainers

bat and ball

Martha's gym shoes

Lunchtime (page 11)

sandwiches

apple

tomatoes

fruit and nuts

cheese

carrot sticks

fork

hot food

knife

banana

Numbers and shapes (page 8)

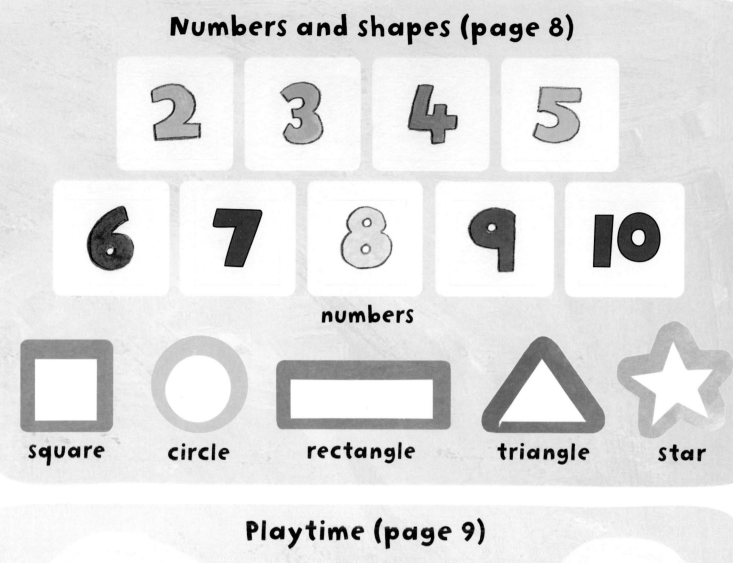

2 3 4 5

6 7 8 9 10

numbers

square   circle   rectangle   triangle   star

Playtime (page 9)

ball   bucket

scooter

rake   windmill   trike   scoop

In the classroom (pages 6 and 7)

ticks for the register

globe

toy cars

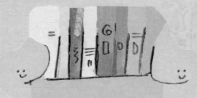

books

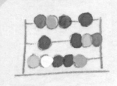

counting toy

blocks

Ruby

Jack

wooden shapes

toy truck

boxes

baskets

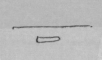

Oliver

Joshua

At the pegs (pages 4 and 5)

Ruby's drink

Ella's backpack

Joshua's backpack

Martha's shoes

Ella's drink

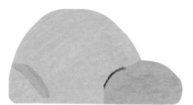

Joshua's hat

Joshua's PE kit

Ruby's coat

Ruby's lunchbox

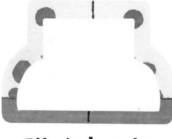

Ella's boots

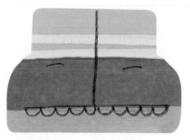

Oliver's boots

Ella's lunchbox

toy car

clock

ball